Can You Tell the Difference?

Is It a Frog or a Toad?

Gail Terp

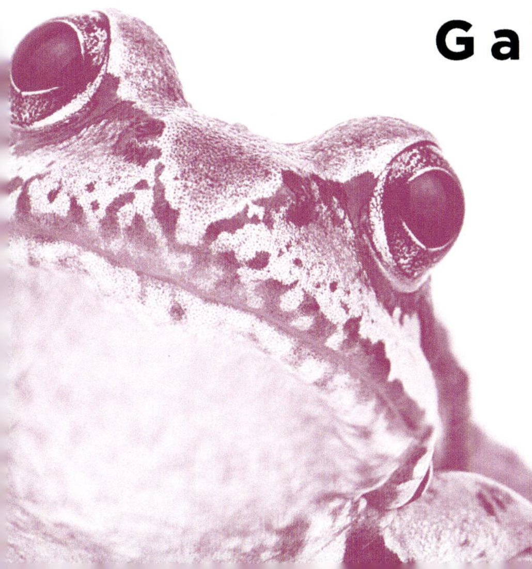

BLACK RABBIT BOOKS

Hi Jinx is published by Black Rabbit Books
P.O. Box 227, Mankato, Minnesota, 56002.
www.blackrabbitbooks.com

Marysa Storm, editor; Michael Sellner, designer;
Omay Ayres, photo researcher

Library of Congress
Cataloging-in-Publication Data
Names: Terp, Gail, 1951- author.
Title: Is it a frog or a toad? / by Gail Terp.
Description: Mankato, Minnesota : Black Rabbit Books, [2020] | Series: Hi jinx. Can you tell the difference? | Audience: Age 9-12. | Audience: Grade 4 to 6. | Includes bibliographical references and index.
Identifiers: LCCN 2018023344 (print) | LCCN 2018025486 (ebook) | ISBN 9781680729061 (e-book) | ISBN 9781680729009 (library binding) | ISBN 9781644660553 (paperback)
Subjects: LCSH: Frogs–Juvenile literature. | Toads–Juvenile literature.
Classification: LCC QL668.E2 (ebook) | LCC QL668.E2 T29 2020 (print) | DDC 597.8–dc23
LC record available at https://lccn.loc.gov/2018023344

Image Credits

Alamy: coroiu octavian, Cover (center frog); Siegfried Grassegger, 12 (toad); Steven Chadwick, 19 (C); Thomas Marent / Rolfnp, 14–15; iStock: AntiMartina, 2–3, 16–17; juliyabrux, 9 (frog), 20, 21 (frog); Shutterstock: Aluna1, 16 (bkgd); benchart, Cover (sky, clouds); Boule, 8 (top); Cathy Keifer, 12 (frog); Christos Georghiou, 7 (center tear), 23 (btm tear); dacascas, 18 (pads); doddis77, Cover (bubble), 1 (bubble), 19 (bubble); ekler, 13; Foto.Touch, 1 (toad); GraphicsRF, 4 (bkgd), 10–11; ilikestudio, 11 (toad); Khvost, Cover (grass); Kurit afshen, 19 (D); Lightspring, 6–7, 23 (frog); Memo Angeles, 4 (frogs, kids), 5 (frog), 10 (cartoon frog); NastyS, Back cover (bkgd), 3, 8 (bkgd), 21 (bkgd); Olexandr Panchenko, 19 (B); opicobello, 7 (corner tear), 17 (tear); Pasko Maksim, Back Cover (tear), 11 (tear), 23 (top tear), 24; Paul Reeves Photography, 19 (A); P Harstela, 8 (toad); pitju, 17 (page curl), 21 (page curl); QiuJu Song, 10 (frog); Ron Dale, 5 (marker stroke), 9 (marker stroke), 18 (marker stroke), 20 (marker stroke); Sarah Holmlund, Cover (left frog); Sarawut Padungkwan, 18 (frog, toad); Smit, 1 (frog); Vitalii Hulai, 16 (toad) Every effort has been made to contact copyright holders for material reproduced in this book. Any omissions will be rectified in subsequent printings if notice is given to the publisher.

Contents

Chapter 1
What Is It?

You're taking a lovely stroll near a pond. Suddenly, a frog or a toad hops onto the path. Curious, you pick it up. It has smooth, wet skin. You really want to take it home. But you've heard about getting warts from toads. Eww. You've also heard about poison frogs. No, thanks! You put it down and rush home to wash your hands.

Was that a frog or toad you picked up? Either way, it's good you set it down. Neither animal enjoys being picked up by strangers. Do you?

A Lot in Common

There's lots to learn about frogs and toads. They look a lot alike. And they're both **amphibians** that live all around the world. (Except Antarctica, that is. It's way too cold.)

It can be hard to tell frogs and toads apart. But this handy guide will help you learn the differences!

Toads do not actually give you warts. (They find this lie very insulting.)

frog

toad

Chapter 2 ALL about Frogs and Toads

Once you know the basic differences, frogs and toads are easy to tell apart. For starters, they tend to be found in different **habitats**. Frogs usually live near water. That's because their skin needs to stay **moist**.

Toad skin doesn't need to stay as moist. Toads still need water, but they can live where it's drier.

The Smooth and the Bumpy

The skin of frogs and toads is definitely different. Frog skin tends to be smooth and wet.

Frogs and toads shed. After shedding, they eat their skin. (Totally disgusting!)

Toad skin is dry and bumpy.
Toads aren't nearly as **sleek** as frogs.

frog

toad

Teeth!

Another way to tell them apart is to peek inside their mouths. If you see teeth, it's a frog. That's right! Frogs have teeth! No worries, though. They can't bite you. Most frogs only have upper teeth. They use them to hold onto their food until they swallow it.

Toads don't have teeth, and they claim to have no use for them. They can hold their food just fine without them.

A group of frogs is called an army. A group of toads is called a knot.

The Joy of Bulgy Eyes

Frogs have **bulgy** eyes. Their eyes can see in front, to the sides, and behind them. Don't you think having frog eyes would be great? Poor toads are not so lucky. Their eyes have no lovely bulge. Scientists believe toad eyes have good nighttime vision.

Frog and toad eyes help push their food down when they swallow. Strange but true!

Leap!

Frogs' long, powerful legs help them leap. Some frogs can leap 20 times their own length. That's like a 10-year-old kid leaping about 90 feet (27 meters).

Poor toads! They have short legs. They can only walk and hop short distances.

Chapter 3

Tell the Difference

At first glance, frogs and toads look a lot alike. But now you know what sets them apart.

A

B

Is it a Frog or a Toad?

C

D

Answers on page 21.

Chapter 4
Get in on the Hi Jinx

People use tools to **predict** earthquakes. But scientists believe toads can do it all on their own. Scientists were studying a knot of **mating** toads. Before the mating season was over, most of the toads left. Five days later, there was an earthquake. The scientists think the toads knew the earthquake was coming and took off. Clever toads!

Take It One Step More

1. Frogs and toads have different types of legs. Why do you think that is? Do some research to find out.

2. What do you think is the easiest way to tell frogs and toads apart?

3. Make a **Venn diagram** using frog and toad features. Do you think they are more alike or different?

A. frog B. toad C. toad D. frog

GLOSSARY

amphibian (am-FIB-ee-uhn)—a cold-blooded animal that can live both on land and in water

bulgy (BUHL-jee)—to stick out

habitat (HAB-uh-tat)—the place where a plant or animal grows or lives

mate (MAYT)—to join together to produce young

moist (MOIST)—slightly or barely wet

predict (pre-DIKT)—to say something will happen in the future

sleek (SLEEK)—straight and smooth

Venn diagram (VEN DAHY-uh-gram)—a diagram that shows the relationship between two groups of things by means of overlapping circles

LEARN MORE

BOOKS

Arnold, Quinn M. *Toads.* Backyard Animals. Mankato, MN: Creative Education, 2018.

Goldish, Meish. *Deadly Frogs.* Envenomators. New York: Bearport Publishing, 2019.

Ryndak, Rob. *Frog or Toad?* Animal Look-Alikes. New York: Gareth Stevens Publishing, 2016.

WEBSITES

American Bullfrog
kids.nationalgeographic.com/animals/american-bullfrog/#american-bullfrog-swimming.jpg

Fowler's Toad
nationalzoo.si.edu/animals/fowlers-toad

Frogs and Toads
www.dkfindout.com/us/animals-and-nature/amphibians/frogs-and-toads/

INDEX